# Start to Learn
# Animals

W

FRANKLIN WATTS

LONDON•SYDNEY

First published in 2013 by
Franklin Watts,
338 Euston Road,
London NW1 3BH

Created and produced by:
Green Android Ltd,
49 Beaumont Court, Upper Clapton Road,
London E5 8BG, UK
www.greenandroid.co.uk

ISBN 978-1-4451-2709-5
Dewey number: 428.1

# Acknowledgements

**Images © dreamstime.com:** bengal tiger © Beetle2k42; falcon © Jordache; komodo dragon © Rokro; lion © Starletdarlene; piranha © Moori; polar bear © F2.

**Images © flpa.co.uk:** blue whale © Richard Herrmann/Minden Pictures/FLPA; leopard corydoras © Gerard Lacz/FLPA; octopus © Brandon Cole/Biosphoto/FLPA; sailfish © Reinhard Dirscherl/FLPA.

**Images © fotolia.com:** atlas moth © ksena32; brown bear © byrdyak; budgerigars © jagodka; butterflies © cynoclub; butterflyfish © bluehand; centipede, emu, poison dart frog © Eric Isselee; chihuahua © zothen; colorado beetle © Marianne Mayer; cuttlefish © Mexrix; dragonfly © M.R. Swadzba; ducks © fotomaster; earthworm © Spencer Berger; emperor moth © JPS; fish © Richard Carey; frog © Sascha Burkard; goldfish © Irochka; goose © DenisNata; goose © yevgeniy11; hens © sval7; labradoodle © biglama; leopard gecko © Thomas Beitz; llama © Vladimir Melnik; millipedes © James Steidl; moreidol © Ian Scott; mosquito © Henrik Larsson; ostrich © sirylok; pangolin © petert2; pig © spinetta; rabbit in a burrow © stanley45; rooster © Anatolii; salamander © Ionescu Bogdan; scorpion © asbtkb; sea slug © Neil Atterbury; seahorse © Onkelchen; seahorse © RbbrDckyBK; stag-beetle © fpainter7; stingray © crisod; tang © aquapix; turkey © Noo; walrus © MAK.

**Images © shutterstock.com:** alligator © Raffaella Calzoni; amazon milk frog, anteater, bearded dragon, chimpanzee, frill-necked lizard, hedgehog with baby, helmeted guinea fowl, hen, king cobra, kookaburra, milk snake, otter, porcupine, rabbit, rabbit and kit, raccoon, red palm weevil, scarlet Ibis, shetland pony, skunk, tomato frog, violet-backed Starling, zebra finch © Eric Isselee; angelfish © Johannes Kornelius; ant © Andrey Pavlov; anteater © Christian Musat; appaloosa horse © Makarova Viktoria; arctic fox © outdoorsman; armadillo © Steve Bower; axolotl, cockatoo © Andrew Burgess; baby Tawny owl © Florian Andronache; bald eagle © Richard Lowthian; bat © Sementer; bee © MPanchenko; bernese mountain dog puppies © steamroller_blues; bernese mountain dog, border collie © Erik Lam; bison © Zack Frank; black rhino © john michael evan potter; blue mountain butterfly © chungking; blue starfish © paul cowell; blue tit © Alexander Erdbeer; blue-tongued skink, jackson's chameleon, tigerfish, veiled chameleon, wood turtle, yellow tang © fivespots; bluejay © Mike Truchon; bongo © Andreas Gradin; brown bear © Jamen Percy; brown snake © Stephen B. Goodwin; buffalo © trevor kittelty; bull © Niar; butterfly © Perig; butterfly on the bark © Wilm Ihlenfeld; buzzard © BogdanBoev; caiman © sohadiszno; camel © alersandr hunta; canaries © ene; cane toad © Chris Ison; cat and kitten © Liliya Kulianionak; caterpillars © Ivanova Natalia, Ziga Camernik; cheetahs © Erwin Niemand, Mark Beckwith; chicks, wood mouse, pig © Tsekhmister; chinchilla © Steshkin Yevgeniy; chipmunk © Tom Reichner; clouded yellow butterfly © jesper skov; clown fish © Sergey Novikov; clown fish, jellyfish © Kletr; cockatiel © Marina Jay; cockroach © seeyou; common toad © Vishnevskiy Vasily; copperhead snake © Rusty Dodson; corn snake © Kruglov_Orda; cows © tarczas; coyote © Birdiegal; crabs © Eugene Sergeev, haveseen; crocodiles © froe_mic, nattanan726; dalmation © Susan Schmitz; deer © Ekaterina V. Borisova; devil scorpionfish © Kristina Vackova; discus © Andrey Armyagov; dolphins © aldorado, Tory Kallman, Paul Vinten; donkey © PD Loyd; duck and ducklings © Ewa Studio; dung beetle © r.classen; eagle-owl © Medvedev Vladimir; eastern collared lizard © Matt Jeppson; echidna © clearviewstock; eel © Pavel Vakhrushev; elephants © Dmussman, Patryk Kosmider; elephant and calf © Four Oaks; emerald tree boa, gecko © ChameleonsEye; emu © S.Cooper Digital; eyelash pit viper © worldswildlifewonders; fairy basslet © Stubblefield Photography; fawn © WilleeCole; fennec fox © Cat Downie; ferret © sbko; fire bellied toad © Michelle D. Milliman; fish © mexrix; flamingo © Atthapol Saita; frog swimming © gradi1975; gaur, hippopotamus, meerkats © tratong; gerbil © Anna Kucherova; gibbon © rujithai; giraffes © Joel Shawn, nelik; golden dart frog © reptiles4all; goldfish © Sergii Figurnyi; gorilla © Rudy Umans; goslings, ginger cat © oksana2010; grasshopper © cristi180884; gray african parrot © Richard Susanto; gray squirrel © Tony Campbell; great crested newt © JGade; great horned owl © csterken; great white shark, elephant and calf © Mogens Trolle; green anole lizard © Leigh Prather; green chameleon © Fedor Selivanov; green fly, wasp © irin-k; green ghromis, cardinal fish © Johannes Kornelius; green iguana © Nneirda; green tree python, victoria crowned pigeon © apiguide; guinea pigs © xstockerx, Vasily Kovalev; hammerhead shark © frantisekhojdysz; hamster © Subbotina Anna; harlequin poison frog, leaf mimic katydid © Dr. Morley Read; hedgehog © Zayats Svetlana; hens © Valentina_S; heron © AngelaLouwe; horse galloping © Olga_i; house spider © Sean Gladwell; hummingbird © kojihirano; humpback whale © David Ashley; ibex, water skater © Vadim Petrakov; iguana © granat; impala © Stacey Ann Alberts; jaguar © stephen; kangaroo © Kristina Postnikova; kangaroo with baby © idiz; kingfisher © assoonas; koala © worldswildlifewonders; korhaan © Daleen Loest; ladybird © Palto; ladybug © Yellowj; lantern fly © takepicsforfun; leaf cutter ant © Micha Klootwijk; leaf insect © kamnuan; leafy seadragon © Joy Brown; leopard frog © Gerald A. DeBoer; leopard shark © AdStock RF; leopard tortoise © Praisaeng; lion © Maggy Meyer; lions fighting © Tobie Oosthuizen; marbled newt © raulbaenacasado; moose, brown bear, storks, leopard, badger © Eduard Kyslynskyy; mossy frog, wood borer beetle © alslutsky; mountain hare © Peter Wey; mouse © Kuttelvaserova Stuchelova; muskox © Cornflower; northern cardinal © Jeffry Weymier; orangutan © Matej Hudovernik; orangutan and baby © Gabriela Insuratelu; orca © Christopher Meder; ornate horned frog, red poison strawberry frog © Dirk Ercken; oryx © Johan Swanepoel; ostrich © Sam DCruz; panda © Hung Chung Chih; parrot © elnavegante; partridges © Mircea BEZERGHEANU; pelican © iliuta goean; penguins © Neale Cousland; penguins diving © Aimee McLachlan; pig © panbazil; pigeon © shuai jie guo; pink dragon millipede © Chatchai Somwat; piranha © Santi Rodriguez; polar bear © Incredible Arctic; polar bear and cubs © Sergey Uryadnikov; praying mantis © Acambium64, Coprid; puffer fish © Kevin H Knuth; puffin © Nicram Sabod; purple sea urchin © NatalieJean; quail © ADA_photo; rabbits © Evgeny Karandaev, Oligo, JIANG HONGYAN; rabbit hopping © Linas T; rainbow lorikeet © jurra8; rat © Pakhnyushcha; red ear turtle © African studio; red Fox © Jeannette Katzir Photog; red panda © feathercollector; red salamander © Cynthia Kidwell; red squirrels © Menno Schaefer, seawhisper; rhino © Leon Marais; rhinoceros beetle © PHOTO 999; ring-tailed lemur © Roberto Caucino; roadrunner © Sekar B; robin © Sebastian Knight; salamander © Arun Roisri; scarlet lily beetle © HHelene; sea turtle © Rich Carey; seagulls © Mrs_ya, Yentafern; seahorse © CHEN WS; shark © prochasson frederic; sheep © Vasilyev Alexandr; sheep and lambs © Eric Gevaert; siamese fighting fish © wimammoth; sika deer © Cologne82; slug, woodlouse © schankz; snail © ahnhuynh; snake slithering © bogdan ionescu; snapping turtle © Carol Heesen; snowy owls © O Driscoll Imaging, WayneDuguay; spider © Kondor83; spider in web © papkin; spotted hyena © Aaron Amat; springbok © J Reineke; squirrel © Shane Wilson Link; squirrel monkey © sohadiszno; starfish © Matthew Gough; stick Insect, earwigs © Melinda Fawver; sturgeons © Maxim Petrichuk; swan and babies © Karel Gallas; swan, mouse © Erni; tabby cat © Tompet; tadpoles © Ronald Wilfred Jansen; tarantula © Aleksey Stemmer; tawny owl © Sue Robinson; tiger drinking © Bill Kennedy; tiger salamander © Gerald A. DeBoer; tiger, puma © Dennis Donohue; toucan, squirrel monkey © Eduardo Rivero; vulture © Sue Green; whale shark © Krzysztof Odziomek; white dove © Tischenko Irina; wolf © Kjetil Kolbjornsrud; woodpecker © schaef71; yak © Im Perfect Lazybones; yellow anacondas © cellistka; yellow crab spider © Henrik Larsson; yellow tangs © Chubykin Arkady, Volodymyr Burdiak; zebras © francesco de marco.

Please note that every effort has been made to check the accuracy of the information contained in this book, and to credit the copyright holders correctly. Green Android Ltd apologize for any unintentional errors or omissions, and would be happy to include revisions to content.

Printed in China
Franklin Watts is a division of Hachette Children's Books,
An Hachette UK company
www.hachette.co.uk

# Note to parents and carers

**Start to Learn Animals** is an exciting way to introduce your child to the animal kingdom. Over 500 colourful photographs will encourage your child to browse through the book, recognising familiar animals and discovering new ones.

Help your child learn the names and groups of many kinds of animals by pointing to the clear labels as you name each animal.

Designed as a fun learning experience, Start to Learn Animals will entertain, as well as educate, young children for many hours.

Colourful photography of animals

Clear labels

Challenging interactive questions

# Contents

# Invertebrates

These cold-blooded animals do not have a backbone. This group includes crustaceans, insects and bugs.

moth

leaf-cutter ant

slug

spider

scorpion

# Birds

These warm-blooded animals have feathers and wings. They lay eggs. Most birds can fly.

dove

woodpecker

seagull

emu

owl

# Reptiles

Reptiles are cold-blooded animals who have scales. They have dry skin and usually lay eggs.

crocodile

lizard

snake

turtle

alligator

# Amphibians

These cold-blooded animals live on land and in water. They have four limbs and moist skin.

frog

salamander

toad

newt

# Fish

These cold-blooded animals breathe underwater through gills. They have scales and fins.

catfish

leafy seadragon

cardinal fish

royal gramma

shark

# Mammals

These warm-blooded animals have lungs to breathe air. They have hair or fur and feed their young with milk.

anteater

elephant

mouse

puma

monkey

oryx

squirrel

orca

Which groups of animals have scales?

# Pets

rabbit

gerbil

mouse

cats

cockatiel

zebra finch

bearded dragon

hamster

guinea pigs

rat

chinchilla

How many of the pets on this page are birds?

dogs

budgerigars

Which of these pets would you like to keep?

goldfish

# Farm animals

bull

Which farm animal do you think is the biggest?

donkey

horse

pigs

ducks

sheep

sheepdog

guinea fowl

llama

cockerel

hens

pony

cows

quail

Which farm animal makes a baa noise?

goat

geese

turkey

# Minibeasts

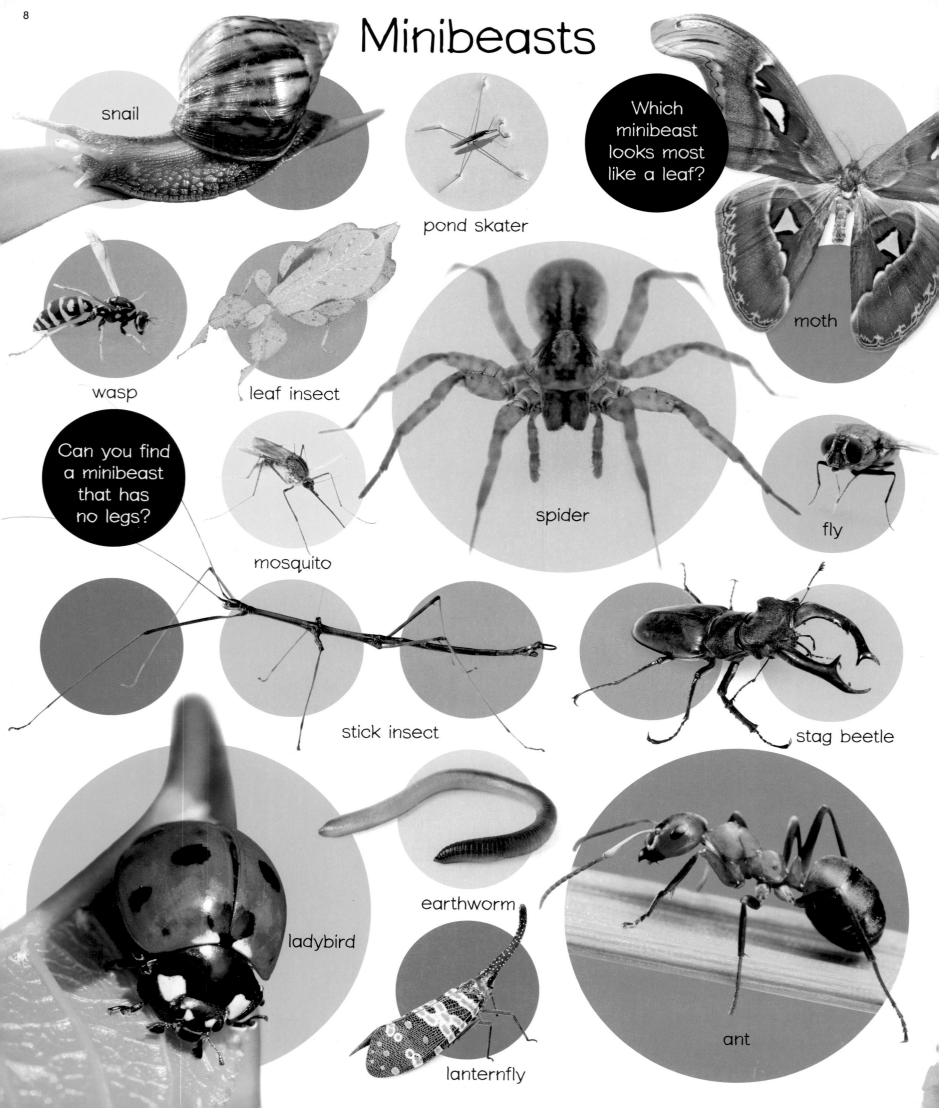

snail

pond skater

Which minibeast looks most like a leaf?

moth

wasp

leaf insect

Can you find a minibeast that has no legs?

mosquito

spider

fly

stick insect

stag beetle

ladybird

earthworm

lanternfly

ant

# Which minibeast has the most legs?

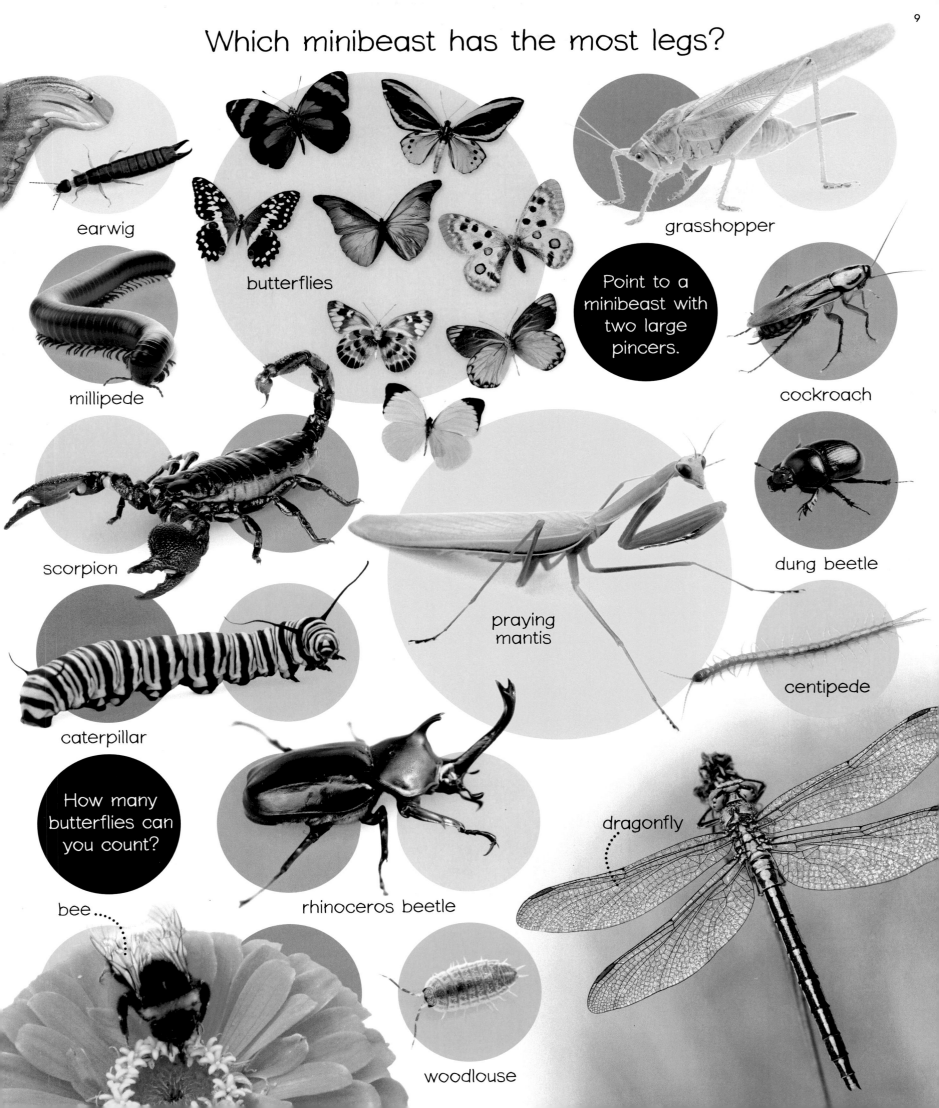

earwig

butterflies

grasshopper

Point to a minibeast with two large pincers.

millipede

cockroach

scorpion

dung beetle

praying mantis

caterpillar

centipede

How many butterflies can you count?

rhinoceros beetle

dragonfly

bee

woodlouse

# Giant animals

hippopotamus

blue whale

Which of these giant animals is a bird?

ostrich

bison

gaur

elephant

brown bear

Which giant animal do you think is the biggest?

# Which giant animal has the longest neck?

Which giant animal has two humps on its back?

polar bear

white rhinoceros

crocodile

moose

How many of these giant animals have horns?

walrus

giraffe

camel

# Superb swimmers

sea lion

tigerfish

whale shark

eel

sturgeon

octopus

rainbow trout

Point to the bright yellow fish.

moorish idol

clown fish

How many tentacles does an octopus have?

sea turtle

damselfish

puffer fish

dolphin

tangs

sailfish

# Which fish has white and yellow stripes?

cuttlefish

lionfish

jellyfish

great white
shark

discus fish

seahorses

butterflyfish

How many
seahorses can
you find?

piranha

humpback
whale

Which animal
is covered in
blue spots?

hammerhead
shark

stingray

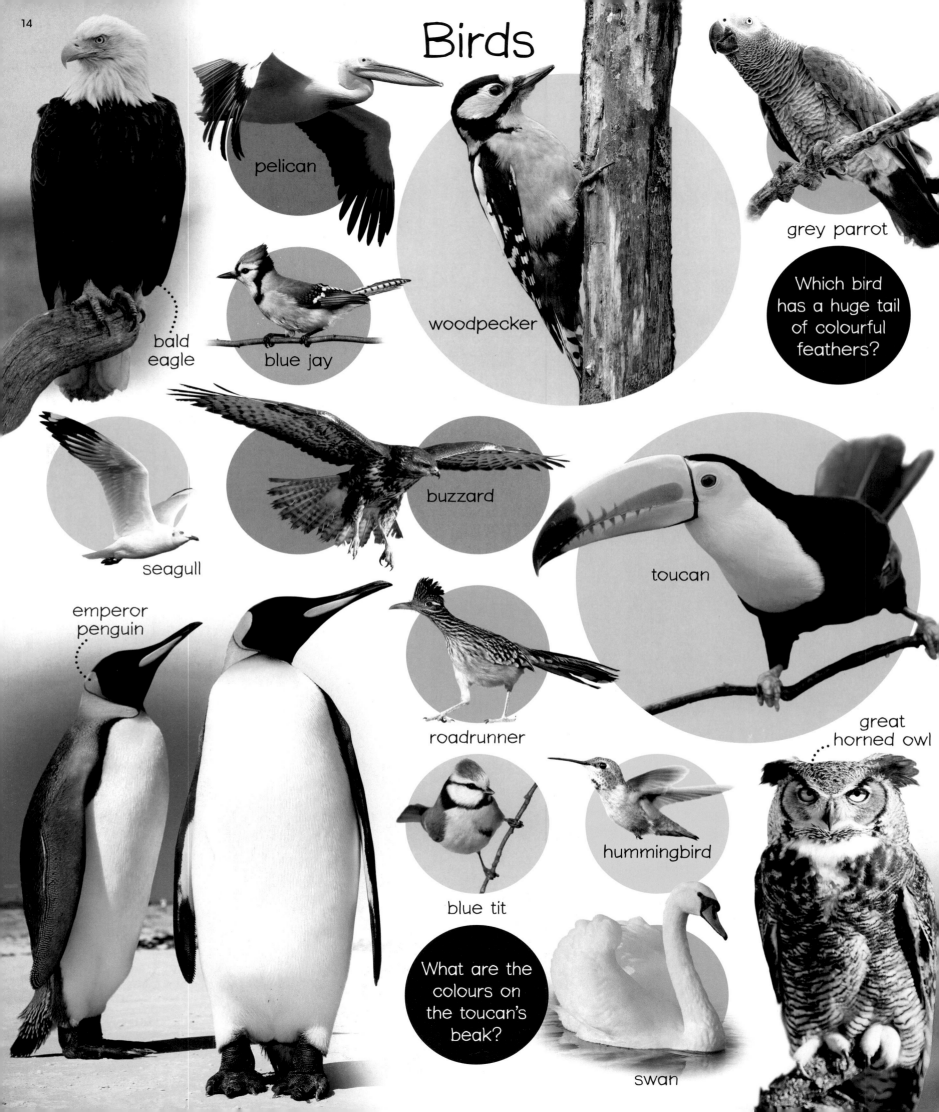

# Birds

pelican

grey parrot

blue jay

woodpecker

Which bird has a huge tail of colourful feathers?

bald eagle

seagull

buzzard

toucan

emperor penguin

roadrunner

great horned owl

hummingbird

blue tit

What are the colours on the toucan's beak?

swan

# Which of these birds do you recognise?

snowy owl

vulture

peacock

peregrine falcon

emu

sparrows

Which birds do you think are unable to fly?

kookaburra

Which birds do you think are the smallest?

cockatoo

pigeon

heron

lorikeet

kingfisher

puffins

robin

# Scaly animals

alligator

corn snake

emerald tree boa

Which scaly animal has a bright blue tongue?

gila monster

frilled lizard

collared lizard

chameleon

anaconda

Komodo dragon

pangolin

iguana

How many snakes can you find on this page?

blue-tongued skink

caiman

Indian cobra

# Horns, spines and shells

Jackson's chameleon

echidna

wood turtle

Which animal do you think has the longest horns?

armadillo

porcupine

African buffalo

snapping turtle

tortoise

crab

ibex

black rhinoceros

hedgehog

Which animals on this page have hard shells?

lobster

# Animals and their babies

owl and
owlet

What is the
name for a
baby horse?

sheep
and lambs

duck and
ducklings

goat
and
kid

Which of
these animal
has the most
babies?

hedgehog
and piglet

deer and
fawn

horse
and foal

dog and
puppies

# Which other baby animals can you name?

polar bear and cubs

Which baby animals look most like their mother?

swan and cygnets

cat and kitten

hen and chicks

kangaroo and joey

rabbit and rabbit kits

goose and goslings

elephant and calf

Which baby animal is in a pouch?

# Furry coats

jaguar

Let's find the three animals with horns.

red fox

gorilla

chimpanzee

brown bear

How many foxes can you see on this page?

impala

otter

muskox

meerkat

hare

yak

fennec fox

# Which furry animal do you think is the smallest?

gibbon

bobcat

Can you find an animal with a stripy tail?

coyote

collared anteater

ferret

red panda

lion

squirrel monkeys

koala

grey squirrel

Which furry animals would you like to stroke?

panda

grey wolf

raccoon

# Camouflage

great grey owl on a branch

devil scorpionfish on a reef

gecko in a desert

Which of these animals is hiding in a pond?

eyelash pit viper on a flower

butterfly on the bark of a tree

korhaan walking in grass

Which animal is camouflaged against the sand?

praying mantis on a leaf

leaf mimic katydid among leaves

frog in a pond

# Which animal is the hardest to spot?

mossy frog on a tree

partridge in a field

copperhead snake on the forest floor

crab on the seashore

green chameleon in a forest

mountain hare in the snow

lion in the grassland

arctic fox in the snow

Point to the animal hiding on a green leaf.

How many of these animals are birds?

yellow
crab
spider

goldfish

Name the
colours of
all the birds'
feathers.

Siamese fighting fish

violet-backed
starling

clouded sulphur
butterfly

blue starfish

pig

caterpillar

scarlet
ibis

Victoria
crowned
pigeon

sea
urchin

Amazon
parrot

Which orange
fish is often
kept as
a pet?

red palm weevil

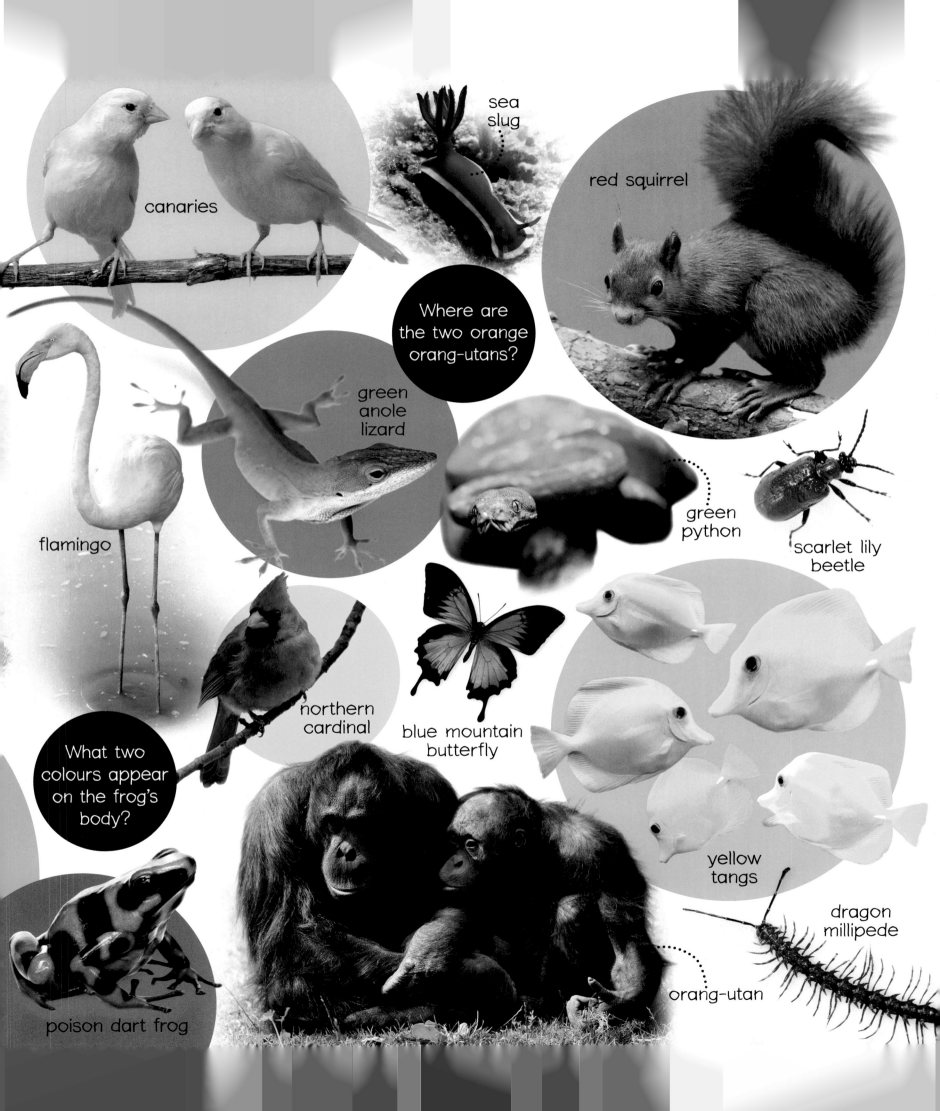

canaries

sea slug

red squirrel

Where are the two orange orang-utans?

green anole lizard

flamingo

green python

scarlet lily beetle

northern cardinal

blue mountain butterfly

What two colours appear on the frog's body?

yellow tangs

dragon millipede

poison dart frog

orang-utan

# Frogs and their family

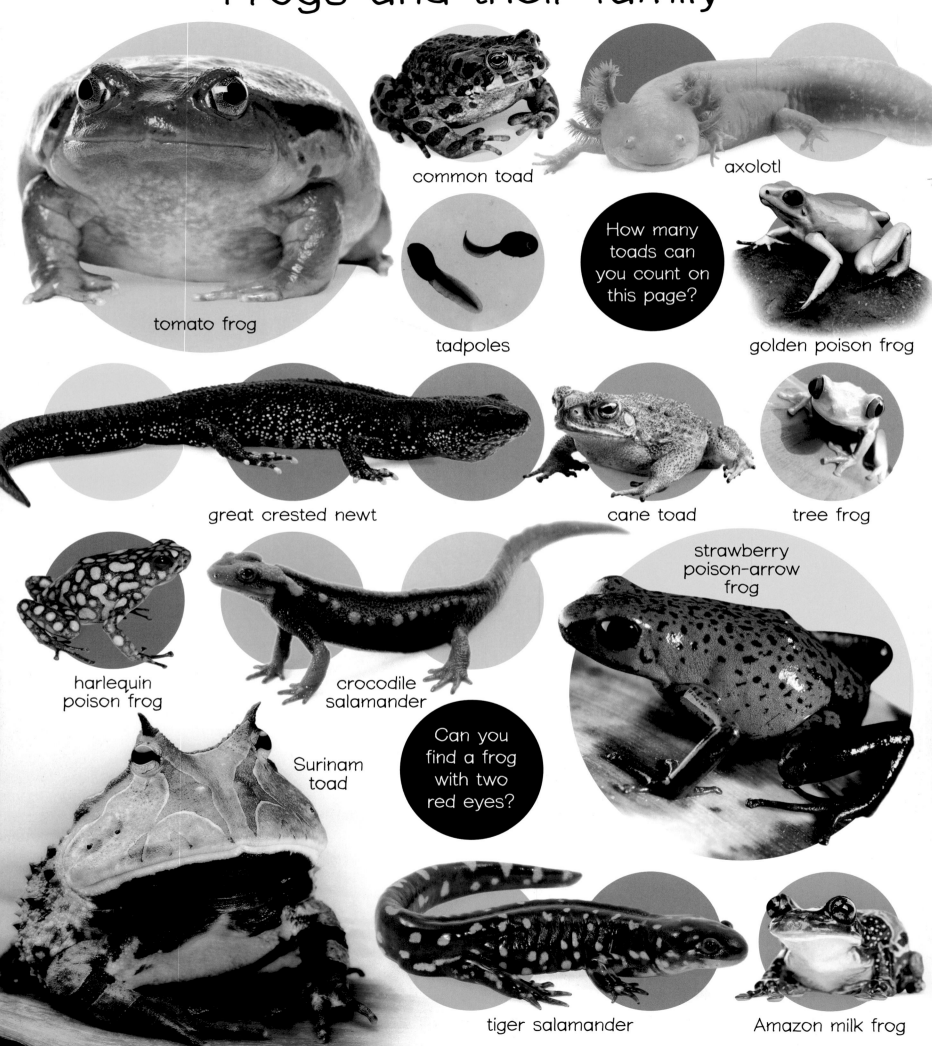

common toad

axolotl

tomato frog

tadpoles

How many toads can you count on this page?

golden poison frog

great crested newt

cane toad

tree frog

harlequin poison frog

crocodile salamander

strawberry poison-arrow frog

Surinam toad

Can you find a frog with two red eyes?

tiger salamander

Amazon milk frog

# Animal homes

storks in a nest

bat in a cave

Which of these animals live in water?

polar bear in the snow

starfish in rock pool

squirrel in a tree

rabbit in a burrow

spider in a web

mouse in a nest

Can you spot the animal hanging upside down?

dolphins in the ocean

Can you name any other animals living in the ocean?

# Spots and stripes

spotted hyena

butterflies

gecko

Where is the butterfly with blue spots?

leopard

bongo

ring-tailed lemur

Colorado beetle

sika deer

leopard frog

Which is the stripy insect on this page?

ladybird

zebra

# Which other spotty animals can you name?

trigger fish

Appaloosa horse

milk snake

skunk

wood borer beetle

How many spots does the wood borer beetle have?

cheetah

angelfish

okapi

Dalmatian dog

chipmunk

caterpillar

leopard shark

tiger

Can you find the spotty trigger fish?

badger

red salamander

# Animals in action

eagle flying

orang-utan swinging

rabbit hopping

fish hiding

tiger drinking

penguins diving

Which animal is spraying water over its baby?

kangaroo jumping

brown bear climbing

elephant spraying water

What type of big cat is drinking water?

snake slithering

# Can you find the orange fish that is hiding?

horse galloping

frog swimming

dolphins leaping

Which two animals are fighting on this page?

cheetah racing

spider crawling

springbok running

hamster washing

giraffe walking

panda eating

lions fighting

Which animal is crawling on somebody's hand?